This Book Belongs to

_____

CHILDREN'S CHOICE®

A Children's Choice® Book Club Edition

GORILLA BABY

The Story of Patty Cake

by Pearl Wolf

PHOTO CREDITS

Barton Silverman/New York Times: front cover, 36; Arthur Sirdofsky: back cover; Edward Hausner/
New York Times: 2, 19, 20; Robert Fitzgerald/Globe: 3, 37, 38, 39; Robert Beach: 8, 9, 10, 15, 16,
23 left, 29, 32; New York Daily News: 13, 22, 23 right, 24. 25, 30, 31, 33, 35 top, 37 bottom; UPI: 14,
26; Lee Romero/New York Times: 18, 27, 34, 35 bottom.

Copyright © 1974 by Pearl Wolf. All rights reserved. Published by Scholastic Book Services, a
division of Scholastic Magazines, Inc.
ISBN: 0-590-75746-6

Printed in the U.S.A.

For Al, Mark and Richard

I wish to thank John Fitzgerald, Director of the Central Park Zoo, and Robert Beach, senior zoo keeper, for their valuable help in writing this book. My thanks also to zoo keeper Richard Regano, who provided much valuable information about Lulu, Kongo, and Patty Cake.

In addition, Dr. George B. Schaller's books *The Year of the Gorilla* and *The Mountain Gorilla: Ecology and Behavior* were essential to my understanding of the gorilla.

Kongo and Lulu are two gorillas who live
in the Central Park Zoo in New York City.

This is Kongo. He is resting in the sun.

This is Lulu. She is going indoors.

Every day people come to visit the gorillas.
Every day the zoo keepers come to feed the
gorillas and play with them.

One day, the zoo keepers see
Lulu holding something.
What can it be?

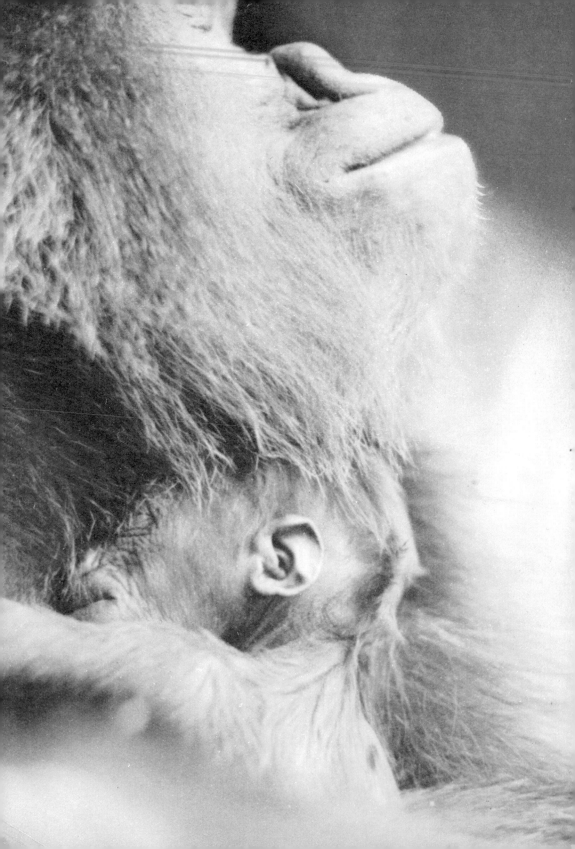

It is a baby gorilla! What a surprise!
No one knew Lulu was having a baby.
It was a secret until this very minute.

See how tiny the new baby is. Gorillas
weigh only about four pounds at birth.
They are smaller at birth than most human
babies. But when gorillas grow up, they
are much bigger than humans. Some gorillas
weigh as much as 600 pounds.

At first, Lulu holds her baby all the time.
She will not let anyone get too close. If
Kongo or the zoo keepers try to come near,
Lulu grunts and even screams to frighten
them away.

For the first few days the zoo keepers think
the baby is a boy. They name the baby Jim.
But then they find out that Jim is ... a ... girl!

Now the baby gets a new name. The zoo keepers
call her Patty Cake.

For the first few weeks Patty Cake sleeps
most of the time. Every few hours Lulu
wakes her and nurses her. Sometimes
Patty Cake cries when she wakes up. She
sounds just like a human baby.

By the time Patty Cake is five weeks old, she is awake much more often. She is getting much stronger. Look at her fingers. See how they hold on to the long hairs on Lulu's body. A baby gorilla has very strong fingers. It must hold on tight to its mother's hair as she swings and climbs. This is the way baby gorillas travel with their mothers in the jungle.

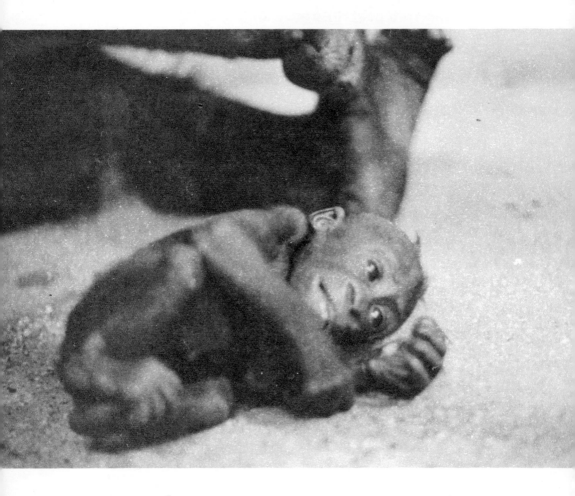

Now Patty Cake is three months old.
She weighs about nine pounds.

She can crawl across the cage. She does not
have to wait for Lulu to come and nurse her.
She can go to Lulu and nurse whenever
she is hungry.

She has some teeth now and likes to taste
some of the food that Lulu and Kongo eat.

At five months, Patty Cake can sit and stand. She can crawl very fast. She can even climb the bars.

But Lulu watches her all the time. If Patty Cake climbs too high or crawls too far away, Lulu goes and gets her. She makes sure Patty Cake is always nearby.

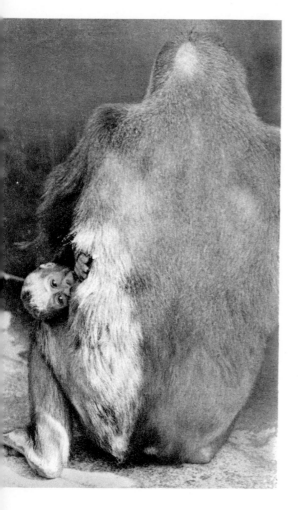

Sometimes Patty Cake crawls to Kongo.
Kongo likes to hold Patty Cake too.

But most of the time Patty Cake stays
with Lulu.

One day there was an accident.

Lulu and Patty Cake were together in one cage. Kongo was sitting in the cage next door. Patty Cake poked one tiny arm through the bars into Kongo's cage. Kongo was holding Patty Cake's hand. But Lulu did not see this.

She took Patty Cake's other hand and began to pull away. Kongo pulled one way. Lulu pulled the other way. That is how the accident happened.

Patty Cake has a broken arm. Now she has to go to the animal hospital in another zoo.

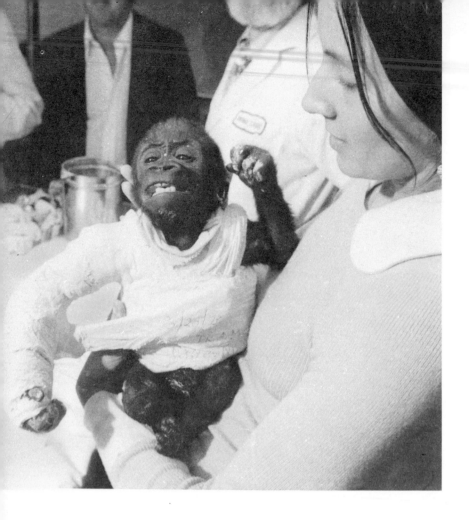

The doctors put Patty Cake's arm
in a cast. The cast goes around her body
to keep her arm from moving. Patty Cake
has to stay in the animal hospital until
her arm gets better.

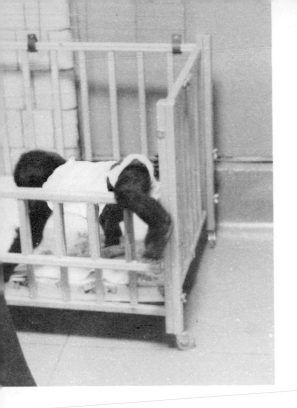
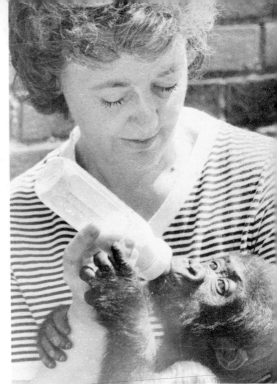

Patty Cake sleeps in a crib at the hospital.
A lady zoo keeper sleeps in the same room.

She holds Patty Cake and plays with
her. She feeds her milk from a baby bottle.

The zoo keeper knows that baby gorillas need
love, just as human babies do.

When Patty Cake's arm gets stronger, the
doctors take off the cast. The zoo keeper takes
Patty Cake outside to play. She gives
Patty Cake lots of toys to play with.

At last Patty Cake is ready to go home. But
will Lulu and Kongo remember their baby?
They have not seen her for three months.
Will they want the baby back? The zoo
keepers do not know.

The zoo keepers put Patty Cake in a cage next to Lulu.
Lulu sees Patty Cake and screams. She knows
her baby. But Patty Cake whimpers. Is she
afraid?

Lulu runs to Patty Cake and touches her gently.
Patty Cake cries. Lulu runs away. But soon
she comes back and touches Patty Cake again.
When Patty Cake stops crying, Lulu picks her
up. She hugs Patty Cake and kisses her and
holds her very close.

Then Kongo comes in. He looks at the baby. He pokes his finger at her gently and then he kisses her.

Now Lulu and Kongo and Patty Cake are together again.

People come to welcome Patty Cake home.
They like to watch the gorilla family.
They like to watch the gorillas eat.

Kongo eats the most because he is the
biggest. Here is what Kongo can eat in one day.
  25 bananas
  20 apples
  15 oranges
  2 large buckets of cereal
  2 quarts of milk
  10 slices of bread
  5 or 6 pounds of different kinds of vegetables

He eats candy, peanuts, and ice cream too.
When Kongo tastes a food he does not like,
sometimes he throws it at the zoo keeper!

Patty Cake drinks milk from a bottle.
When Kongo and Lulu see this, they want
bottles too.

Here is Kongo drinking apple juice.

When they are not eating or resting, the gorillas like to play.

Lulu and Kongo like to wrestle. Sometimes they beat their chests and roar. Gorillas do this when they get excited. It makes them look fierce, but they are really peaceful animals.

Patty Cake likes to swing and climb.

Kongo likes to be squirted with the hose.

Lulu likes to shake hands with the zoo keeper.

She likes to untie the zoo keeper's shoelaces.

Now Patty Cake is one year old. She is having her first birthday party. The zoo keepers bake her a big banana cake.

All the children who come to the zoo get birthday balloons. They bring Patty Cake presents and birthday cards.

And everyone sings "Happy Birthday" to Patty Cake— the little gorilla baby who was born in the zoo.